HIT and RUN

Barbara Mitchelhill

Published in association with
The Basic Skills Agency

Hodder & Stoughton

A MEMBER OF THE HODDER HEADLINE GROUP

Acknowledgements
Cover: Steinar Lund/Illustration Web
Illustrations: Maureen Carter

Orders: please contact Bookpoint Ltd, 130 Milton Park, Abingdon, Oxon OX14 4SB. Telephone: (44) 01235 827720, Fax: (44) 01235 400454. Lines are open from 9.00–6.00, Monday to Saturday, with a 24 hour message answering service.

British Library Cataloguing in Publication Data
A catalogue record for this title is available from The British Library

ISBN 0 340 86944 5

First published 1999
This edition published 2002
Impression number   10 9 8 7 6 5 4 3 2 1
Year   2007 2006 2005 2004 2003 2002

Typeset by Fakenham Photosetting Ltd, Fakenham, Norfolk
Printed in Great Britain for Hodder & Stoughton Educational, a division of Hodder Headline Plc, 338 Euston Road, London NW1 3BH by Athenaeum Press, Gateshead, Tyne & Wear.

Contents

1

The Strangers

It was late one afternoon
last winter.
I saw them looking
at our house.
A boy and a girl –
about my age.

2
Do I Know You?

––––––––––

'Do I know you?' I said.
'No,' they said,
'but you will.'
Then they walked away
into the dark.

3
New Neighbours?

I told my sister, Lucy.
'Maybe they live
down our road,' she said.
But I had never
seen them before.

4

Outside School

The next day,
I saw them again.
They were waiting for us
outside school.
'We'll walk home with you,'
they said.

5
Nearly Home

We were half way
down May Lane.
We were almost home
when a red sports car
came round the bend.

6
Look Out!

'Look out!' I said.
But the boy and girl
didn't move.
The car ran through them
as if they were made of mist.

7

Ghosts?

We were scared
and we ran home. Fast!
We couldn't believe
what we had seen.
'G-ghosts!' said Lucy.
'B-but where
have they come from?'

8
There Again

The next day, Lucy and I
saw them again.
They were standing
in the middle of May Lane.
We were scared
but we walked towards them.

9
The Headline

_____

This time, the girl
held up a newspaper
and I saw the headline:
'Hit and Run Driver
Kills Teenagers in May Lane.'

DAILY NEWS

HIT AND RUN
Driver Kills
Teenagers
in May Lane

10
Who Was Killed?

'Were you killed in May Lane?'
Lucy asked.
But they shook their heads.
Then, in a flash,
they both vanished.

11
Why Tell Us?

_____

'Why tell us
about a hit-and-run?'
I said. 'It's a horrible thing to do,'
said Lucy.
'We have to walk down here
every day.'

12
A Warning?

As soon as she said it,
the idea came to me.
Of course!
The ghosts had come to warn us.
We were the ones in danger.

13

The Red Sports Car

Suddenly, I heard a car.
Then the red sports car
came round the bend.
'Look out, Lucy!' I yelled.

14
Hit and Run

———————

I flung myself
on to the grass.
The red sports car
went shooting past me.
It didn't stop.
It didn't even slow down.

15
No Reply

I could hardly breathe.
My head hurt
and my leg was bleeding.
'Lucy!' I yelled,
but there was no reply.

16

Oh Lucy!

When I looked up,
I saw her.
She was lying
in the middle of the lane.
She wasn't moving at all.

17

The Ambulance Arrives

Somehow, I got to a house
and called for help.
An ambulance came –
but it was too late.
Lucy was dead.

18
The Headline Again

When I saw the newspaper
the next day, I felt sick.
'Hit and Run Driver
Kills Teenager in May Lane.'
The ghosts' warning
had saved me –
but not my sister.